Laike and Nahum

A Poem in Two Voices

Canada Council   Conseil des Arts
for the Arts   du Canada

The publisher gratefully acknowledges the support of the Canada Council for the Arts for its publishing program.

Library and Archives Canada Cataloguing in Publication

Panofsky, Ruth
  Laike and Nahum : a poem in two voices / Ruth Panofsky

(Inanna poetry and fiction series)
ISBN 978-0-9782233-1-1

1. Jews, Russian – Québec (Province) – Montreal – Poetry.
2. Immigrants – Québec (Province) – Montreal – Poetry. I. Title. II. Series.

PS8681.A644L33 2007   C811'.6   C2007-902140-9

Cover/Interior design by Luciana Ricciutelli
Printed and bound in Canada

Inanna Publications and Education Inc.
operating as *Canadian Woman Studies/les cahiers de la femme*
210 Founders College, York University
4700 Keele Street
Toronto, Ontario M3J 1P3
Canada
Telephone: (416) 736-5356 Fax (416) 736-5765
Email: inanna@yorku.ca Website: www.yorku.ca/inanna

Laike and Nahum

A Poem in Two Voices

RUTH PANOFSKY

Inanna poetry & fiction series

INANNA Publications and Education Inc.
Toronto, Canada

Although inspired by the lives of my maternal grandparents who emigrated from Russia to Montréal early in the twentieth century, this poem has assumed a shape of its own, separate from the real individuals whose names it invokes. This work is the product of my imagination; speakers and events bear little more than a passing resemblance to actual individuals and the circumstances of their lives.

For Gary
advisor and confidant

Contents

PART ONE

Laike

1

You arrive
with the hardened mud
of Russia
on your boots –
foreign gait
light touch

> *I*
> *a girl*
> *barely sixteen*

2

My aunt pays
for your passage
to *Amerike*
offers welcome
hope
in a new tongue
and quiet
at dusk

freedom
belated

3

Caution
Mother warns
against the brusque
stranger
feet planted
on the floor
back straightened
to the wooden chair
eyes intent
on the smallest detail
of antimacassar
on the shabby couch

I enter
avert my eyes
Mother's words
ring in my ears

4

Dare I speak cousin
lift my eye
to your gaze

willing exile
from your knowledge
of Cossack terror
my parents'
burning antipathy

here we meet
in secret
share a tongue
a lineage
a desire
that brings
us to this place
again

5

You open
to me
you do not know
your own heart
but you come
with grace
or guile
you come to me

6

You recall
the brutal threat
of official gesture
banishment
into army service
your hardened youth
emptied of hope

7

Avoid the greenhorn
Father inveighs
settled emigré
he shuns you
as he shuns
his former self
newly Canadian
he wants more
for his daughter
than the stern Bolshevik
who courts her
with awkward grace

8

You promise nothing
have nothing to offer
but your constancy
yet each evening
when you come
to claim me
I step forward
stand at your side

9

You lighten days
dampened by
faint hope

in your proud gait
the future
is weighted
with promise

10

White shirt after white shirt
starched and pressed
the scorching iron
heavy in your hand
steam searing your face

did you cross oceans
for so little?

11

You are bold
stake your life on me
evenings
we walk together
through the city
say little
exchange fears

12

I yield to your touch
as you discover yourself
in the folds
of my skirt
my softening hands
Laike Lily
my English name
awkward on your tongue

13

I colour
the grey canvass
of your world
mute the iron's hiss
the boss's spit
each evening
when you return to me
purging pain
with my promise

14

Without shame or fear
I share the secret
of your child
to be born in spring
and you are pleased
bound to a future
to me

15

Mother rages
and Father glowers
knowing
that poverty
beckons

you are buoyed
by my calm
at rest in my arms

16

We marry at dusk
under a linen canopy
my parents move aside
as I take your hand
we accept the rabbi's blessing
celebrate
having found
quiet joy
together

17

In the back room
of my parents' flat
our son is born
in rending pain
I deliver him
into the small dark
world of our making

I
a mother
at seventeen

Nahum

1

On the sea voyage
I am too sick to think
of Kuzmin
of *tateh* and *mameh*
left behind
illness cleanses me
leavens my fear

I am made anew
aboard a cargo freighter
bound for *di goldene land*

2

I arrive to
the glare
of strangers
the callous soul
of an alien city
church spires in regular view
a commingling of languages
tease the ear

Oh, how my tongue aches
for lucid speech
the hard cadence of Russian
still ringing in my ear
as I assault
brute *Eng-lish*

Ba-na-na
I practice
and bite into the hard
yellow peel of the fruit
only to spit it out
in disgust

the waxy pulp
stuffs my mouth
shut

3

There is no dignity
in the work
none
the foreman
spews foreign words
that rack my ears
I grasp
his meaning
work harder still
Russian lout

4

Amid blinding steam
and the hiss of irons
I press
shirt after laundered shirt
counting mindlessly
eyn   tsvey   dray
until the brief break
when my lunch bucket
betrays me
to the glare
that poverty brings

salted herring with onion
ripe tomato   coarse cheese
on black bread
the steaming strong coffee
will not assuage
dank heart
damp brow

5

Fingers form
a perpetual grip around
the solid weight of iron
the buffeting haze of
heat and steam
small comfort

6

You are my cousin
you are my love

When we meet
île Mon-tré-al
opens to me
I stroll the streets on Sunday
and the brisk air inspires
I breathe in the cold
deeply
embrace this city
of work
of promise
of you

7

A recurring dream:
floating amid feathers
shards of glass
refract a sun's
meagre rays
the haunting dirge
of lowing cattle
a village bereft
Kuzmin mayn Kuzmin
I moan

8

From across the room
I court you in silence
my body is open
my spirit willful
I've come for you
I now know
I've come only for you

9

The press of the past
will not abate

I awake nightly
to rallying cries
Beat the Jews and save Russia
the silent slashing
of knives
tearing through towns
and the lives
of young men
who dream a future
in places unknown

10

I am coarse
you call me bold
I am ignorant
you hear wisdom in my thoughts
I am poor
you see my promise
I am myself
and you find that enough

11

Haunted
by years of soldiering
among loathing Cossacks
the only passion I know
is hatred
yield slowly
to your gentle offering
of love

12

Your mother scorns me
for your pregnancy
the shame it brings
she cannot know
that I was yours
the moment
I entered your parlour
and you saw me
with a tenderness
I had never known
and soon
it was right
for us to share
a knowing passion
a fathoming of souls

13

No shot-gun wedding this
you are my bride
in spirit and flesh
with you
I am whole

14

You are weary after
Jacob is born
and there is no privacy
in the back room
of your parents' flat
where we steal space
to be a family

nightly they rail
a galling cad
a husband of no means
Oh Laike Laike
how dare he claim you

soon we move
to the soothing silence
of private rooms
and pray
my small earnings
will hold

Part Two

Laike

1

Our rooms are cramped
cold
the baby grows healthy
at my breast
a boy borne for you

2

The euphoria
of privacy
passes

long hours
alone
with the baby

I await
your return
past dusk

3

The dark
Depression years
when you are angry
for lack of work
are hardest

your stoic heart
lacerated will
wound me

4

The children
come in
quick succession
one girl among
five boys

she is coldest
of all   ·

5

Palate dulled
plate bare

I struggle to keep
children healthy
and sated

levity is starved
by deprivation
and shame

6

Offered promotion
to foreman
you refuse
this burden of responsibility
for another's wife and children

and your family, Nahum
what of us?

7

Your pride
you say

I take strangers
into these rooms
feed them
scrub this filthy flat clean
transform rags into
shirts for the boys

my only daughter
turns from me

what pride have I, Nahum?

8

At midnight
we flee the flat
and the landlord's demands
take refuge up the street
in another set of rooms

three times in three years

9

Hannah goes to school
in Jacob's shirt
and the teacher jeers
how shameful
what disgrace

Hannah's stone cold heart

10

I offer succour
to my only daughter

she turns away

11

Lazar at two
falls to his death
from our balcony

Hannah at five
watches him land
on the concrete

I at thirty-two
warm soup
at the stove

12

Six children
minus one

I count
and count again

Five boys
Jacob, Isaac, Abraham, Lazar, Saul
and one girl
Hannah

One is missing
gone

13

Dreams of children
plummeting
through pitch of night
buried by dawn

conjure the ghost
of Lazar
tiny among boys
grown tall and bold

14

Five boys and one girl
                  one boy missing
                  small boy

light and noise
of a hospital corridor
disrupt my rest

                  two flights up
                  iron balustrade

the nurses are kind
they calm me
with pills
and soothing words
chère Madame, ces mauvais jours will pass
they will pass, Madame
dormez, Madame, dormez

                  two flights up
                  iron balustrade
                  Hannah watching
                  Lazar falling

five boys, one girl
                  one boy missing
                  small boy

15

Hannah   my daughter
will you not love me
a little?

> *Let me be, Ma*
> *just let me be*

16

The keening of
sick women
in hospital
frightens you

Laike   bist dir gezunt
can I bring you something
please get well my Laike
dear Got
make her well

17

We move one last time
to a ground floor flat
no balcony
no climbing
no falling
no

Nahum

Without work
I eat little
sleep less
rail at the world
that offers me
nothing

2

Winter
bread lines
and soup kitchens

heart beats
cold
in my chest

3

Children
need food
always more food

4

Nahum   Nahum
he's falling
catch
catch him

anguished cries
disrupt
sleep

across
a divide
of dream
and death
I touch
your arc
of loss

5

Your fall
follows Lazar's

I lose wife
son
self

6

Coroner confirms
death upon impact

free of suffering

splayed on sidewalk
crushed forehead
bruised cheek
broken limbs

a boy of two
breaks easily
on concrete

the weight
of suffering
crushes
a man of forty

7

You are deep
in darkness

among the ghosts
of motherless boys

I await you
at the surface

breath halted

8

You and Hannah
share grief
imprinted
in concrete

9

Grateful
for your return
I take a vow
of grace

Laike
share my breath

10

The Party promises
fancy pressers
jobs
at union wages

I dream collars
and cuffs
pressed smooth
with dollar signs

enough
to feed family
pay the landlord
his due

11

Synagogue whisperings
of crematoria
stir memories
of Kuzmin

imprint
terror

12

Acrid fumes
from Hitler's ovens
drift overseas
seal the fate
of brothers
left behind
in Kuzmin

death camp blood
spills over
Cadieux Street

maudits Juifs

13

On the street
the boys scuffle
Hannah too
a feisty fighter

our will
now theirs

Part Three

Laike

1

The older boys marry
in quick succession

Saul studies
in the back room
of the rental
on Hutchison

Hannah returns
from work
spent
happy

youngest son
only girl
sheltered
home

2

Hannah indulges
a longing
for cashmere

shade of apricot
sets off
her dark eyes

without her
wages
we could not manage

3

Belated bride
at twenty-nine

Hannah flees
to the suburbs

seeks refuge
in the tiny hold
of a brick bungalow

secures herself
within

4

Charring pain
rends the telephone wires

Hannah's sobbing
sears my heart

strikes me
dumb

5

Shards
of language
amid anguish

> *vos*
> *are the girls okay*
> *are you okay*

I long to whisper

> *come home*

6

He's beating the kids

Hannah cries into the phone

I am silent

numb

7

On Sunday visits
I look for signs

bruises
cuts
marks

see nothing
say nothing

8

Hannah calls again

I offer
no words
of comfort

9

She says
he beats the girls
Nahum

           vos sugst dir
           no
           can't be

10

Hannah
is it true

her look
aghast

11

Nahum
what to do
or say

shunned for so long
I fear her need

12

She grows
accustomed
to attack

hatred
hardens
my heart

13

I defied
tateh and *mameh*
for you, Nahum

tonight
mayn tokhter bends
to a brutal husband

my
legacy

14

Nahum
I cannot bear

much   more
                    veytik

must shun
            can't she see

I hurt
            too

so many years
            without a daughter

and now she wants

                    Nahum
bear   cannot
                        pain
more
            no

15

Yielding
gradually
to grief

I mourn the loss
of parents
son
daughter

my past
unearthed

embalming
relief

16

At your urging, Nahum
I write

my dear Hannah

can you ever
forgive my silence

proffer succour
the solace of words
long withheld
mother's embrace

17

A cup of strong tea
at the formica table

Hannah accepts
this offering

of grace
and renewal

Nahum

1

After overtime
at the factory
I return to
a quiet house

Sam at night school
Hannah at work

You and I
alone
after many years

2

The foreman admires
collars, cuffs, seams
starched and ironed
to perfection

Nat, you are
a master

my Russian pride
roused

3

Lacking the will
to foreman others

I decline
the offer

strive
to please
myself

4

A practiced presser

careful craftsman

my hand
grips the iron

slowly draws down
across each shirt

steady release
of steam

5

What do you mean
he beats the girls

vos heyst – beat

a slap on the behind
like I gave Saul
when he stole bread
from the bakery

like I gave Hannah
when she answered
me sharply

vos heyst beat

does it mean
with fists

does he hit them

with fists

6

Laike

tell her to come home
to us
with the girls

tell Hannah
we will manage

somehow

7

Abject daughter
distraught wife

cast together
in sorrow

divided by silence
united in grief

8

At Sunday dinner
my eyes
meet Hannah's

they seek hope
offer refuge

she turns away

9

Hannah warns

> no, Pa
> don't say anything

> we'll be fine
> I'll see to it

I hold my tongue

its secret lashings

> ikh bist keyn tateh
> no father at all

10

In moments of great joy
or deep sorrow
we seek one another

bound by
resilience

the torment
of years

11

Solace
a bracing walk
in evening chill

the company
of *landsmen*
at synagogue

grandchildren
playing

and you, Laike
long my wife

12

With each
pressed shirt
the suffering
subsides

memories
of Kuzmin
mameh and *tateh*
brothers gone

losing Lazar
your grief
and Hannah's sorrow

distilled, released
through the
soothing, searing
steam

evanescent
dispersed

13

Enough, Laike
you must yield
to your daughter

I will
the pardoning
of souls

14

Your hand
reaches

across the
dinner table

to rest gently
on Hannah's

15

Laike
I yearn for you

recall
the heat of
summer evenings
when we
made love
freely

soft kisses
sweetened lips

bold passion
subdued fears

were we not brazen

Laike
ikh veln dir

16

You read
tea leaves
at the kitchen table

see a happy future
promise goodness

Hannah softens
turns toward me

> *you see, Pa*
> *I told you*
>
> *if Ma says,*
> *it's true*

Yiddish Glossary

Amerike	America
bist dir gezunt	are you okay
di goldene land	the land of gold
dray	three
eyn	one
Got	God
ikh bist keyn tateh	I am no father
ikh veln dir	I want you
landsmen	countrymen
mameh	mother
mayn	my
tateh	father
tokhter	daughter
tsvey	two

veln	want
veytik	pain
vos	what
vos heyst	what does it mean
vos sugst dir	what are you saying

Acknowledgements

I am indebted to Jacqueline Borowick and Merle Nudelman, writing colleagues whose incisive comments helped refine my work. This book has benefited from the invaluable research advice offered by Jesse Aaron Cohen and Hermann Teifer of the Center for Jewish History, New York; the staff of the Dorot Jewish Division, New York Public Library; Janice Rosen of the Canadian Jewish Congress Charities Committee National Archives, Montréal; and Eiran Harris and Shannon Hodge of the Jewish Public Library, Montréal.

This book has been supported by a Ryerson University Creative Fund Grant. An early, abbreviated version of Part One appeared in *White Wall Review*.

Born and raised in Montréal, Ruth Panofsky lives in Toronto where she teaches at Ryerson University. Her first volume of poems, *Lifeline*, appeared in 2001. She is also the author of several scholarly books, most recently *The Force of Vocation: The Literary Career of Adele Wiseman*.